STEP-BY-STEP

Flowercraft

By Eunice Svinicki

Golden Press • **New York**

Western Publishing Company, Inc.
Racine, Wisconsin

One good way to dry and preserve plants is to hang them upside down. This method ensures straight stems and upright flower heads.

Art Director: Remo Cosentino
Art Assistant/Diagrams: Diane Wagner
Editor: Caroline Greenberg
Assistant Editor: Evelyn Stone
Photographs: George Ancona

Library of Congress Catalog Card Number: 76-55117

Contents

Introduction

The arts of flower arranging and flower making are as old as our appreciation for flowers. They provide us with the opportunity to use our sense of design and composition, our knowledge of texture and color, our imagination, and our love of nature.

One of the most fundamental aspects of flowercraft is the gathering and arranging of fresh flowers and natural materials. Once mastered, the basic rules for arranging fresh flowers can be applied to any sort of flower, whether it be freshly picked, dried, or constructed out of anything from paper to cloth to metal. Because dried flowers and foliage can be used to create beautiful arrangements with long life spans, this book discusses the gathering and preserving of a wide variety of natural materials, including flowers and plants, fruits, vegetables, fungi, seedpods, and cones. It contains information on how to make traditional fresh flower arrangements and instructions for using dried flowers in many other ways as well—mounting them in frames, printing with them, decoupaging with them, embedding them in plastic, and making collages with them. It even contains recipes for fragrant potpourris and sachets, pomanders, powders, and colognes.

The fundamentals of flower making are also explained in this book, along with instructions on how to craft a variety of artificial flowers from paper, fabric, and natural materials. And a section on arrangements for special occasions provides directions for making festive wreaths, centerpieces, garlands, swags, and corsages.

As anyone who loves flowers knows, there is an infinity of uses for them, both fresh and dried. The projects and examples found throughout this book will serve as an introduction to the wealth of possibilities in the world of flowercraft.

(Facing page) The black-eyed Susans, daisies, Queen Anne's lace, and yarrow for this arrangement were preserved in cornmeal and Borax. Pottery by Marilyn Much.

Bittersweet, artichokes, eucalyptus, and cross sections of pine cones —dried naturally and arranged on driftwood

Vegetables can be used to make handsome arrangements, too. Here, a large cabbage serves as the container for celery, peppers, dill, radishes, broccoli, and carrots.

Natural Materials

The garden, the fields, and the woods are just some of the sources from which you can obtain materials for arranging and preserving flowers and foliage. Nature offers a boundless source of materials, but you must be prepared to search for them, bearing in mind what function they will serve—that is, as elements for a fresh flower arrangement, or as materials to be dried or preserved and used later on.

Cultivated flowers are an obvious choice for fresh or dried arrangements. Remember that the entire flower does not have to be used. The centers of daisies or dahlias, the pods of eucalyptus, or the leaves of the magnolia can be used in themselves as part of an arrangement. Any part of a plant—buds, leaves, petals, calyx, or seedpod—is useful material. Cultivated grains, such as wheat and rye, are excellent for establishing the basic line of any design. Like cultivated fruits and vegetables, they can be used fresh in arrangements, and then dried according to the methods described in the following chapter and used again. Pomegranates, pineapple tops, artichokes, ears of corn, okra, poppy pods, the leaves of purple cabbage, beets, and horseradish can all be used in this way. Herbs such as dill, sage, thyme, rosemary, and parsley make wonderfully fragrant arrangements which can be dried for later use in cooking, or for making potpourri.

Wild plants, including flowers, cones, pods, berries, grasses, and weeds, can be used fresh and then dried, or used after they have dried naturally outdoors. Wildflowers, such as goldenrod, Queen Anne's lace, daisy, and milkweed, are especially beautiful, and can be found in abundance in many places. Cones from evergreens, though traditionally used in holiday wreaths, are attractive at any time of the year. Clusters of berries, such as bittersweet and sumac, work well as the focal point of many designs, and they retain their color after being dried. Cattails, grasses, wild grains, gourds, and nuts, even cacti, thistles, and thorns make interesting additions to fresh or dried arrangements. No matter where you live, you will find that the list of materials is nearly endless once you have begun to look around you.

GATHERING NATURAL MATERIALS

Before beginning a plant collecting trip, become as familiar as possible with plants that are considered rare or endangered species. In addition, learn to identify common poisonous plants, such as sumac, poison ivy, and poison oak, so that you can avoid them.

If possible, gather plant material on a dry day, after the sun has evaporated the morning dew. Unless you want plants in a particular stage of development, such as in bud, gather them just as they become mature. Never tear at a plant or branch with your hands; always use a sharp knife or kitchen shears so that you can cut the stems cleanly.

Tie the flowers together in bundles, or lay them out singly in a carton with tissue paper between each layer. If you are gathering plants that wilt quickly, wrap the cut stems in wet paper toweling kept in a plastic bag.

Drying and Preserving Methods

Flowers, foliage, and other natural materials such as herbs, vegetables, grains, and grasses can be preserved in many ways. One way is to remove their moisture, by hanging them, pressing them, or burying them in a granular drying agent. Other methods involve treating them with preservatives or chemicals, such as glycerin, wax, or bleach. The method you use will depend on the type of plants you choose and the space and time available to you. Once you have read the information on the various preserving methods, you will have a better idea of which one to start with.

HANGING

One very simple and effective way to air-dry plants is to hang them upside down. This method ensures straight stems and upright flower heads—plants dried upright in a container, on the other hand, will droop.

While many plants will fade or turn to a neutral or brown color when dried by hanging, some will retain their color quite well when dried in this way. Color retention is best if the plants can be hung in the dark. The following is a list of some of the flowers that can be dried successfully by hanging. Those marked with an asterisk retain their color especially well.

Acacia*
Baby's breath*
Bells of Ireland
Cattails* (gather in early summer)
Celosia*
China aster*
Clematis*
Delphinium*
Goldenrod
Hydrangea
Japanese lanterns*
Lavender
Mimosa*
Queen Anne's lace
Rhodanthe*
Strawflowers* (pick these and other flowers with papery petals just
   before they bloom; they will open while hanging)
Yarrow

Grains and grasses may also be air-dried by hanging. Some berries, such as sumac and bittersweet, may be picked fresh and hung to dry. Herbs should be harvested at their prime.

Remove leaves from flowers and tie your plants together securely in small bunches. Hang them in a dry room (basements are usually too damp) from the ceiling, a clothesline, or a drying rack, so that air can circulate freely through them.

If space is limited, tie the bunches to a coat hanger and hang them in a closet. If you are drying herbs that will be used for cooking purposes, a paper bag should be tied around the herbs to keep dust off them while they are hanging. To avoid rodent problems, hang grains from a nail in the center of your attic, or the ceiling of a closet.

Check the plants periodically and retie if necessary so they won't fall. Let them hang until they are stiff and crisp—about two or three weeks— and then take them down carefully.

At this point you may wish to preserve the plants further by spraying them lightly with an aerosol varnish, but this is not strictly necessary. If you do not use them right away, store the dried plants upright in large jars or flat in boxes. Group like materials together. Treat them carefully, as they will be rather delicate and brittle.

PRESSING

Pressing flowers is extremely easy, and pressed flowers can be used in many interesting ways: mounted in frames, as decorative elements in collage and decoupage, and in the making of greeting cards, to name a few. Colors will be retained at almost their original hue if the flowers are pressed correctly.

Flowers that aren't especially thick work well for pressing, as do grains, grasses, and leaves. Very fleshy flowers or leaves should not be pressed.

Basically, all you need to press flowers is some absorbent paper, such as newsprint, and some heavy weights, such as books, records, or bricks. (Floral suppliers, listed on page 64, sell special absorbent paper for pressing flowers, as well as flower presses.)

Lay flowers down between several thicknesses of paper, and then place your weights evenly on top. If you are pressing a great many flowers, stack them on top of each other between layers of paper. Change the paper every day for the first four or five days to help maintain the color of the flowers. To press a flower with a high center, such as a daisy, place the blossom on a piece of newsprint, and then cut a hole the size of the flower center from a second piece of newsprint and place it on top of the blossom.

Most plants take approximately one month to press.

GRANULAR DRYING AGENTS

Granular drying agents, such as silica gel, Borax, silica sand, and beach sand, preserve flowers quickly and efficiently (though they don't work well for green foliage), and little or none of the flower color is lost.

Silica gel is not a gel, but rather a lightweight granular substance that works more quickly than any of the other granular agents, and seems to preserve flower color more efficiently as well. (Silica gel is available at craft stores and gardening centers.)

Borax, the granular cleaning powder, can be used as a drying agent in combination with cornmeal. The manufacturer suggests using their

Pressing. Lay fresh flowers between layers of newsprint and stack heavy weights on top. Change the paper every day for the first four or five days. Press until flowers are flat and completely dry—about one month.

Using Granular Drying Agents

1. Granular agents such as Borax and cornmeal, or silica gel, preserve flowers quickly, with little color loss. (Other preserving methods, such as soaking in glycerin, are better for foliage.)

2. Insert a length of wire up through the head of flat-headed flowers such as daisies. Bend the end of the wire over to form a hook and pull it gently back into the head of the flower.

1

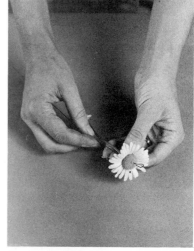

2

3. Twist the wire down the stem to strengthen it.

4. Place flat-headed flowers *face down* in drying agent (stem up). Remove stems from dense, multi-layered flowers and place flower heads *face up* in agent. (Add a wire stem after drying; see picture on page 11.) Sprinkle agent over and around the flowers, using just enough to cover.

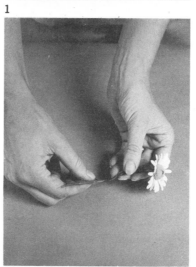

3

4

5. When flowers feel crisp and dry, remove them from the drying agent and brush off excess grains with a soft-bristled brush.

6. If any petals have fallen off, glue them back on.

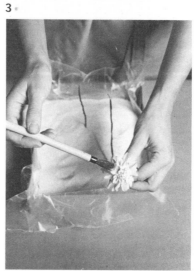

5

6

product for this purpose in a ratio of one part Borax to two parts cornmeal.

Silica sand is an extremely fine, lightweight sand.

Beach sand, too, may be used as a drying agent. It should be sifted carefully first, then washed, and then dried thoroughly in the oven; if it is at all damp it will spoil the flowers. Since beach sand is heavier than other granular drying agents, it should be used only on rather sturdy flowers.

Since successful flower preserving is in some part a matter of personal experimentation, you may find that the efficacy of a particular drying agent varies from one plant to the next, or that a combination of agents works better than a single one in some cases. You may wish to experiment with drying agents such as cornstarch, talc, alum, salt, or pet litter, as well as the ones mentioned above.

Almost all flowers may be dried using this method; single blossoms work especially well. Since green foliage doesn't dry well in granular agents, you may want to replace or reinforce the stems of the flowers with wire. Stalky stems may be removed before drying, treated in glycerin, and then wired back on to the dried blossoms.

To use granular drying agents, line a sturdy container, such as a cardboard box or a plastic tray, with waxed paper. Pour about half an inch of the agent into the container. Strip all foliage, except the leaves around the flower head, from the stems of your flower.

Place flat flowers, such as daisies, face down (and stems up) in the container; stems should be reinforced by twisting fine wire around them. Place multi-layered flowers, such as dahlias, face up, after removing their stems; wire stems can be added after the flower heads have dried. You may lay stalky flowers, such as snapdragons, on their sides, or remove the flowers from their stems. Do not crowd the flowers, and use a separate container for each kind.

Using a spoon, pour a small amount of the drying agent under the petals of the flower so that it maintains its natural shape. Do this carefully. Pour just enough of the agent into the box to cover the flowers, since too much of the agent will flatten the flowers. Do not cover protruding stems. Label the box with the date and the type of plant, and store it in a dark, dry place.

Drying time for all agents except silica gel is about one week; silica gel takes from one to five days, depending on the density of the flowers.

If you are not sure how long your flowers should be left in the agent, use one flower as a test flower, and check on it from day to day. When it feels dry and crisp, the flowers are ready to be removed from the agent. If the least bit of moisture remains in the flowers they will wilt. Over-drying will result in brown spots.

Brush flowers off with a soft brush to clean away the drying agent. (If petals fall off as you remove flowers from the agent, save them and glue them back on later.) Add a wire stem to stemless flowers by pushing a thin piece of wire into the head of the flower. A dot of glue will hold wire stems in place. Faded petals may be painted with diluted acrylic paint or watercolors.

After drying, insert wire through the head of stemless flowers. Bend the end of the wire over to form a hook and pull it back into the flower.

Most granular agents can be used many times. After you have removed flowers from the agent, let it dry, and if it is lumpy, sift it through a wire screen. Silica gel has blue indicator crystals that turn pink or white when the silica gel has absorbed too much moisture. To dry silica gel for reuse, put it in a slow (200 to 300 degree) oven until the indicator crystals turn blue again. Do not use the silica gel until it has cooled.

GLYCERIN

Glycerin in solution is used primarily to preserve foliage. Unlike granular drying agents, it causes a change in plant color (colors will darken or turn brownish); however, it has the advantage of preserving foliage so that it remains soft and pliable. Foliage treated with glycerin can be used indefinitely, either in dry arrangements or in combination with fresh flowers in water.

To use glycerin (available at any drugstore), make a solution of one part glycerin to two parts hot water; mix well. Pour the solution into a container tall enough to hold the foliage stems; use enough solution to cover the stems to a depth of at least two inches. Bruise the end of each stem (crush with a hammer) so that the glycerin can be absorbed more easily. Place the foliage in the container, making sure that the solution reaches two to four inches up the stems, and leave it there until the glycerin has been absorbed into the leaves. Preserving time varies with the thickness of the plant tissue. Some plants take only a week, while others need two to three weeks. Foliage is ready when it has changed color completely and feels pliable and soft.

Save any solution which has not been absorbed; it can be reused.

Although leaves that have been soaked in glycerin change color, glycerin-treated foliage remains pliable, and can be used in both dry and fresh arrangements.

WAX

A coating of wax applied to leaves will preserve them without changing their color, and the leaves will last indefinitely. This preserving method is especially good with colorful autumn leaves. It is almost impossible to wax fresh flowers because the wax is warm and usually causes the flowers to wilt. However, flowers can be waxed after they have been dried.

One way of waxing leaves is to dip the entire leaf into melted paraffin or candle wax and hang it up by its stem until the wax has hardened. Hang the leaves over newspaper.

Another way to wax leaves is to press them, using waxed paper: Place the leaves between the waxy sides of two sheets of waxed paper, and then place newspaper under and over the waxed paper. Press with a hot iron. Pressed flowers can also be waxed this way.

BLEACHING

Certain leaves, such as fern or ti leaves, can be used to dramatic effect in flower arrangements after they have been bleached. To remove the chlorophyll, or green coloring matter, from leaves, immerse them in a solution of one cup of bleach to one gallon of water for two to four hours, or until the green pigment has been removed. Be careful not to over-bleach or the plant will deteriorate. Rinse the leaves gently with clear water and dry them on absorbent paper. When the leaves are completely dry, preserve them in glycerin or press them by weighing them down between sheets of absorbent paper.

DRYING GOURDS

Dried gourds make a colorful addition to dried flower arrangements, especially those featuring fall foliage.

Harvest gourds just as they mature, wash them with soap and water, and prick a tiny hole in the end of each one. Place them on a cooling rack or hang them by their stems with string or wire in a cool, dry place for at least two months. You will hear the seeds inside the gourd rattle when the gourd is completely dry.

If a shiny finish is desired, dried gourds may be treated with paste wax, clear varnish, or shellac. They may also be painted or stained.

DRYING CONES AND SEEDPODS

Though cones are most often used in floral arrangements during the Christmas season, they are effective in arrangements at any time of the year. They can be picked before they are fully mature; drying and heating will cause them to open and increase in size.

To dry cones, scrub them with soap and water to remove pitch and then place them in a shallow box in a cool, dry place. If you wish to dry them quickly, sit them on a radiator or place them in a warm oven.

Seedpods can be dried in various ways. They can be allowed to dry out on the tree or plant, or they can be picked green and then air-dried. To air-dry seedpods, hang them upside down by their stems, or place them on a flat surface in a warm place. They, too, may be dried quickly in a warm oven.

Dry pine cones in a warm oven until they open and increase in size.

Principles of Flower Arranging

The basic principles and techniques of flower arranging discussed here and in the following chapter apply to preserved and simulated floral materials as well as fresh ones. You will want to take as much care in arranging dried or fabricated flowers as you would a fresh bouquet.

COLOR, TEXTURE, SHAPE, AND COMPOSITION

Flower arranging is a visual art based on the elements of color, texture, shape, and composition. Some familiarity with each of these elements is an invaluable asset when planning an arrangement, for each of them plays an important part in the arrangement's final effect.

Color. Knowing colors and how to use them to their best effect is an art in itself. In the most basic way, colors generate feelings and emotions: reds, oranges, and yellows, like fire and the sun, suggest warmth, while greens and blues, like water and foliage, are cool and placid. Since nature provides us with the entire color spectrum, a knowledge of color principles is helpful in guiding our choice of color combinations.

The three primary colors are red, blue, and yellow. All other colors are made from mixtures of the primary colors.

Pure colors are called *hues*. The *intensity* of a color refers to its brightness or dullness. A color can be made lighter or darker by adding black or white to it. A *tint* of a color is made by adding white to the color; pink, for example, is a tint of red. A *shade* of a color is made by adding black to it; blue-black is a shade of blue. A *tone* is the result of adding both black and white to a color.

Colors are customarily arranged on a color wheel. They include the primary colors, namely red, yellow, and blue; the secondary colors, green, orange, and purple; and the intermediate colors, red-orange, yellow-orange, yellow-green, blue-green, blue-purple, and red-purple.

Color schemes, or harmonies, have been developed out of this systematic arrangement as guidelines for color planning. The most common color harmonies are listed below.

Monochromatic—which makes use of only one color, in combination with any of its tints, shades, or tones.

Analogous—which uses colors that are adjacent on the color wheel, such as blue with blue-green and green.

Complementary—which uses colors that are opposite each other on the wheel, such as red and green.

Split complementary—which uses a color and the two colors next to its complement on the wheel, such as purple with green and orange.

Triad—which uses three colors that are equidistant from each other on the wheel. Triads are often composed of one full intensity color and tints, shades, and tones of the other two colors.

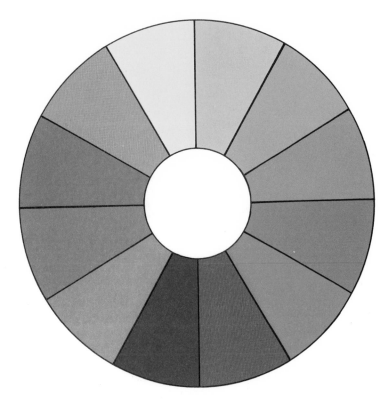

Use the color wheel as a guide in determining color schemes for your floral arrangements.

Neighbors on the color wheel (for instance, blue and violet) are used in analagous color schemes. Complementary schemes use colors that are opposite each other on the wheel (such as red and green). A monochromatic scheme is made up of tints, shades, and tones of one hue (for instance, light yellow, gold, and lemon yellow).

A floral design is a carefully planned composition. The arrangement on the right is more effective than the one on the left because basic principles of flower arranging were followed—and a container properly proportioned to the floral display was used.

Texture, an important element in floral design, should always be considered when planning an arrangement. Contrasting textures can add interest to even the simplest arrangement. Notice, too, how texture can affect the overall design. For instance, an arrangement using brightly colored flowers can still look soft if flowers with velvety or soft petals are used—such as pansies or roses. The use of materials that are lacy and fragile, such as baby's breath or fern fronds, will add an element of delicacy to a large arrangement.

Shape is another important element in flower arranging. The most common shapes used in floral designs are the crescent, the Hogarth or S-curve, the round, the oval, the triangle, the vertical, and the horizontal. (The mechanics of assembling each of these shapes is discussed in the following chapter.)

Composition is the element in flower arranging that ties everything together and gives it unity. Factors such as proportion, balance, repetition, and emphasis come into play when any flower arrangement is being composed.

The proportion of flowers and foliage in relation to their container has a great deal to do with how the arrangement looks. The container you use should neither overpower the arrangement nor be too small for it, and it should, of course, be suitable for the flowers it holds. Generally, in vertical arrangements, the height of the arrangement should be one-and-a-half to two times the height of the container. In horizontal arrangements, the height of the arrangement should be one-and-a-half to two times the width of the container.

Every flower arrangement should have balance—that is, the weight of the arrangement should look evenly distributed. A line is visualized through the center as a check to see whether one side looks heavier than the other. Since dark colors appear heavier than lighter ones, they are usually placed near the center and base of the arrangement, while light-colored and smaller flowers are arranged at the top and sides.

Repetition helps to unify the composition of an arrangement. Thus, the color of the container is repeated in the colors of the flowers, or a color is repeated in two different kinds of flowers (yellow daisies and yellow marigolds, for example), or the type of flower or foliage used is repeated many times in the arrangement.

Arrangements are given emphasis with a focal point, which may be one particularly beautiful flower, a bunch of small, brightly colored flowers, or an interesting dried vegetable, gourd, or cone. The focal point of the arrangement is generally placed at the center bottom, with the other flowers and foliage arranged around and above it.

CONTAINERS

The container you use for your arrangement can be anything from a gilt vase to a piece of driftwood. Of course, for fresh arrangements you will need a container that holds water (or you will have to use a jar or a tin can inside the container). For dried or fabricated arrangements, your choice is even wider. Since the container you choose will affect the look of the arrangement, it should be suitable for the flowers and foliage you use, its shape and size should be scaled to the size of the flowers and foliage, and its surface and texture should harmonize with the materials

There's no need to be limited to vases when displaying flowers—all kinds of holders can be used. The examples here show unusual settings (the coffee grinder and the shell), an arrangement under a glass dome, and a miniature design in the bowl of an antique spoon.

Unique containers enhance these dried arrangements. (Top right) A crocheted holder. (Bottom right) Pottery vases by Mary Ann Olsen. (Below) Suede vase. Directions for making this unusual container, which holds a natural arrangement of thistles, grasses, lotus pods, and tansy, are given on the opposite page.

it will hold. Delicate sweetheart roses, for example, would look better in an antique sugar bowl than they would in a tall Oriental vase, while an arrangement of dried grasses and wildflowers would look better in an earthenware crock than in a crystal vase.

Certain types of containers are better suited to particular types of floral designs than others. Round bowls, for example, look best with round or oval floral designs. Tall cylindrical containers look best with vertical designs, including the Hogarth or S-curve type. Flat containers are most appealing with triangle, crescent, and horizontal arrangements, while urn-shaped containers are suited to oval, round, and triangular designs.

When looking for the appropriate container, do not limit yourself to flower vases, but take into account such household items as pitchers, sugar bowls, kitchen mugs and canisters, earthenware crocks and jugs, goblets, baskets, old wooden boxes, metal boxes, small wooden drawers, handmade pottery, and interesting bottles and fruit jars. Tin cans, painted or wrapped with fabric, seashells, gourds, and driftwood are additional possibilities. For dried arrangements (which don't require containers that hold water), you might even crochet or weave a small holder, or make the suede vase described below.

Suede Vase

Materials

assorted scraps of suede
bond typing paper (2 sheets)
carbon paper
rubber cement
cardboard tube or can
scissors
pencil

Directions. Cut both sheets of bond paper to fit around the cardboard tube or can. Draw a free, meandering line design on one of them. Use carbon paper between the two sheets of bond to transfer the design on the first sheet to the second sheet. Number the duplicate shapes on each sheet.

Cut out one shape at a time from one of these numbered pattern sheets and use it as a guide to cut the shape out of suede. Apply rubber cement to the corresponding shape on the uncut pattern sheet and place the suede shape in position. Continue to cut the shapes out of suede and rubber cement them in place on the uncut pattern sheet. The edges of the suede should butt together, not overlap.

Cement the suede-covered sheet to the cardboard tube or can. Finish the top with a strip of suede cemented to the rim. If necessary, use sand or some other weight in the bottom of the vase to prevent it from tipping over.

Add a bouquet of dried weeds to complement the rugged texture of the suede.

Wire can be used to curve the stems of flowers for Hogarth or crescent-shaped floral arrangements.

FLORAL DESIGNS

Your choice of a floral design should be influenced by the type of flowers and foliage at hand, whether they are fresh, dried, or fabricated, the size and shape of your container, and where you intend to put the arrangement.

There are two broad classifications of floral designs. Mass, or traditional, arrangements tend to use a great deal of plant material, and often consist of many small flowers around a focal point of large flowers. Line, or modern, arrangements tend to be simpler than mass arrangements, and are characterized by a spare, restrained, linear look.

For the purposes of flower arranging, most flowers and foliage can be classified as line, focal, or fill materials.

Line flowers and foliage are generally tall and slender, and are used to establish the line of the arrangement. Florist's wire may be used to curve line materials for use in Hogarth or crescent-shaped arrangements.

Some excellent line flowers and foliage are: pussy willows, snapdragons, Bells of Ireland, eucalyptus, wild grasses, grains, gladioli, goldenrod, delphinium, celosia, and cattails.

The focal point of an arrangement is the center of interest, the point from which the lines of the design radiate. It can be the largest of all the flowers in full bloom, a bunch of flowers that are brighter in color than the others, or a large group of small flowers. Some good focal materials are: hydrangeas, magnolia blossoms, artichokes, clusters of any small flower, seedpods, daffodils, dahlias, geraniums, and chrysanthemums.

Fill materials are used to fill in the spaces around the focal point and the line of the arrangement. Modern line arrangements make little use of fill materials; traditional mass arrangements use them in quantity.

Pictured below (from left to right) are examples of various plant materials that can be used to: establish line, create a focal point, and fill in an arrangement.

Most types of foliage, and flowers such as baby's breath, sweetheart roses, starflowers, Queen Anne's lace, and bittersweet, are all excellent fill materials.

This triangular design of fresh daisies, tansy, goldenrod, and Queen Anne's lace, arranged by Vicki Fredericksen, is a mass arrangement.

Techniques of Flower Arranging

MATERIALS

The following is a list of useful tools for working with both fresh and preserved floral materials.

Holders are used to hold flowers and foliage in place in an arrangement.

The frog is a glass disk perforated with evenly spaced holes. It works well for fresh arrangements of flowers with thick or woody stems.

The pin holder is a heavy metal holder whose top is covered with small metal spikes. The spikes are close enough to hold heavy stems as well as small ones.

The mesh holder, like the frog, is suitable for flowers with thick or woody stems.

The line arrangement here is a simple, restrained design composed of spider mums, cabbage leaves, and dill.

Chicken wire can be crumpled up to fit inside almost any kind of container to hold stems in place. It is especially useful for odd-shaped containers, and for tall ones.

Florist's clay can be used to hold dry or simulated flowers in place, or to anchor holders to containers. (Fresh flowers wilt when put in clay.)

Plastic foam works well for dry arrangements. Some plastic foam comes with an adhesive backing, so that it can be stuck directly to the container.

The oasis is similar to plastic foam, but can be soaked in water and used with fresh flowers.

Plasticine, or modeling clay, like florist's clay, can be used to hold dry arrangements or to secure holders to containers.

Floral tape is a green, self-sticking adhesive tape used to disguise wire stems or to bind fresh flower stems together. Fresh flowers with prickly stems are sometimes bound in floral tape.

Floral picks are used to strengthen weak stems. The pick consists of a length of wood sharpened at one end, with a piece of wire at the other end. The pick is held alongside the stem and the wire is wrapped around both. Picks can be used to extend stems as well.

Aluminum wire comes in various gauges and has various uses: 18-gauge wire is stiff and works well as artificial stems for crafted or dried flower heads; 24-gauge wire is flexible and can be used for wrapping around natural stems to reinforce or curve them, for holding parts of arrangements or crafted flowers together, and for attaching ornaments to floral displays. **Florist's wire,** which is green, may be used whenever aluminum wire is called for.

Tape adhesive is a sticky tape with paper backing that is used to anchor holders to containers.

Pole pins are U-shaped pins that are used to fasten foliage or stemless material to an oasis or to plastic foam. Hairpins, similar in shape, may also be used for this purpose.

Stem cutters are excellent for cutting heavy stems or wire stems.

Kitchen shears or **pruning shears** are used to cut fresh flowers and foliage.

PREPARING FLOWERS FOR ARRANGING

Fresh flowers. Strip away all foliage that will be covered by water to avoid decay. Cut stems on a slant to permit water absorption; crush heavy, fleshy, or woody stems with a hammer. Some flowers whose stems contain a milky juice will last longer if the stems are seared in a flame; do this with poppies, dahlias, hydrangeas, zinnias, and ferns.

Line materials that will be used in Hogarth or crescent-shaped arrangements can be curved by either wrapping with florist's wire (see picture on page 20) or by inserting wire carefully through the length of the stem, and then bending it.

Dried flowers. Plants that are to be dried and used later in curved arrangements can be tied to pre-shaped wire so that they will dry in the shape desired.

Use floral picks to extend stems.

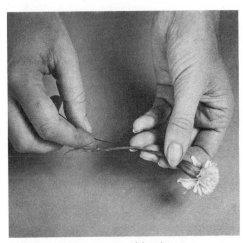

Reinforce weak stems with wire.

Use floral tape to cover wire-reinforced stems. (*Note:* The above methods work best with dried materials.)

Use florist's clay or tape adhesive to anchor holders to containers.

When using an oasis, cut it slightly larger than the container and push it in *wet*. Pull off excess from sides.

PREPARING CONTAINERS

Thoroughly clean the flower holders and containers you are going to use and let them dry. Anchor flower holders to your containers with florist's clay or tape adhesive. Put a small wad of clay on the bottom of the holder and press it firmly into the container until it is secure. Then place strips of clay or adhesive around the edges of the holder to secure it further. (If the holder shows after the arrangement has been completed, you can cover it with foliage, moss, or pebbles.) In working with lightweight, dried, or fabricated materials, it may be necessary to weight your container with sand to prevent it from tipping over.

ASSEMBLING YOUR DESIGN

When you are ready to begin arranging, gather your materials together and clear a working space. Cover your work surface with newspapers for easy cleanup. Work at eye level.

First, decide which floral shape you want to make, and if it is to be a mass or a line arrangement. Mass arrangements can be made in any of the basic design shapes (illustrated on the facing page), but line arrangements work best in vertical, Hogarth, or crescent shapes.

In all designs the skeletal shape or length of the line should be one-and-a-half to two times the height or width of the container (whichever is greater).

The three basic steps in putting together any flower arrangement are:

1. Establishing the basic outline of the design
2. Securing the focal flowers
3. Filling in with fill flowers and foliage

Crescent. Secure line flowers which have been curved to form a crescent shape (see page 23). Add focal flowers to the center, just above the base. Using smaller flowers and foliage, fill in around the focal point and up the crescent slightly.

Horizontal. Secure the line flowers extending out on either side of the container so that flowers and container form a horizontal line. Secure focal flowers in the center. Fill in around the focal point.

Triangle. For an equilateral triangle shape, place one line flower upright in the center of the container to establish the height of the arrangement. Place two line flowers on each side of the center flower to form a triangle with sides of the same length. Place focal flowers in the center, allowing them to drop slightly over the top of the container. Fill in with foliage and smaller flowers, keeping them inside the triangle's boundaries.

For a right-angle triangle shape, first place line flowers in the container to establish the height of the arrangement. Secure other line flowers on either the left or right side to delineate the outline. Secure focal flowers at the base of the triangle and fill in, maintaining the outline.

Vertical. Secure a line flower in the center of the container to establish the height of the design. Place focal flowers at the base so they hang over the top of the container slightly. Fill in with foliage and flowers, maintaining the vertical shape of the arrangement.

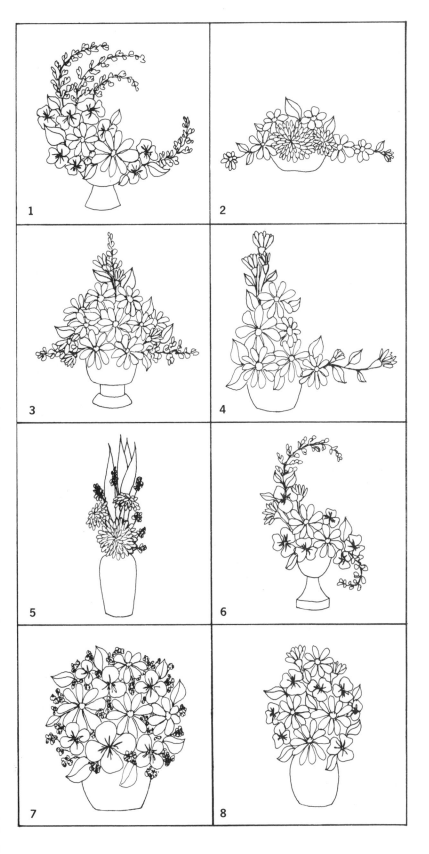

Basic Design Shapes

1. Crescent
2. Horizontal

3. Triangle (equilateral)
4. Triangle (right-angle)

5. Vertical
6. Hogarth or S-curve

7. Round
8. Oval

For a Hogarth design, arrange pre-curved line materials in an S-shape. Add one or more focal flowers. If desired, fill in with smaller flowers and foliage, following the curve of the line materials. Always keep in mind the concepts of proportion, balance, repetition, and emphasis when arranging a display.

For an equilateral triangle design, use line flowers to establish the height and base of the basic triangle shape. Arrange focal flowers in the center. Fill in with smaller flowers and/or foliage. (See the example on page 21.)

Hogarth or **S-curve.** Place curved line flowers (see page 23) in container to form an S-shape. Add focal flowers to the center, but arrange them so that they follow the curve slightly. Fill in with foliage and smaller flowers if desired.

Round. Round and oval arrangements contain no line materials, and are often made with only one kind of flower and one kind of fill. Arrange several flowers into a ball shape in the center of the container (each flower should extend out the same distance from the container). Use more of the same flowers to fill in the ball shape. Fill in with smaller flowers or foliage.

Oval. Arrange flowers so that they are higher at the center than at the sides. Add more of the same flowers to fill in the oval outline, and fill with foliage or tiny flowers.

Special Occasion Arrangements

Decorative arrangements can add a feeling of festivity to special occasions throughout the year. An attractive centerpiece is a delightful table ornament whether it be for a summer barbecue or a Thanksgiving dinner; a swag of flowers will create an air of gaiety at an outdoor spring party, while a garland of evergreens can brighten your living room at Christmastime. Striking displays can be made in any season using fresh, dried, or crafted materials and a bit of imagination.

In winter, when fresh flowers are scarce in many parts of the country, seasonal displays are popular. Evergreen branches, celosia, Scotch broom, magnolia leaves, and poinsettia flowers are just some of the materials that may be used to establish line and shape in a winter arrangement. Good focal materials are seedpods, pine cones, and holly berries. Containers you might consider include old kerosene lamps or lanterns, silver or pewter jugs, boxes covered with gift paper, or hollowed logs. These are often used in combination with candles, or with Christmas decorations such as candy canes and glass balls.

Evergreens can be attached directly to a plastic foam base; since greens have thick stems, use pole pins to secure them. When making a centerpiece, work with a piece of plastic foam that is big enough to ensure a sturdy arrangement, and be sure to cover it completely.

Here, greens were wired to an old lantern to create a striking wintertime display.

Pine cones of various sizes and types are mixed with whole nuts in an impressive wreath by Mrs. Tom Schloegel.

A straw wreath, by Marilyn Wieting, decorated with grasses, strawflowers, and ribbon

Pine cone wreath. Use a saber saw to cut a circle out of plywood. Use a putty knife to affix materials with linoleum paste.

Straw wreath. Cover plastic foam base with crumpled newspaper and then wind with masking tape. Lay small bunches of straw around the circle and wire in place.

Wreaths, though traditionally made of evergreens, can also be made of grasses, cones and nuts, straw, or any number of other materials. Almost any item—a bow, a bunch of dried berries, candy canes—can be used as an accent or focal point.

A sturdy wire circle is needed for wreaths made of evergreens or dried grasses. A heavy wire coat hanger can be fashioned into a circle, with the hook used for hanging, if the materials to be hung on it are light enough. For large wreaths, galvanized wire is essential to prevent sagging. Use fine wire to secure the materials to the frame, being sure to wire them firmly enough to prevent them from slipping around the frame. Wear gloves to protect your hands.

To make a wreath of materials such as cones, seedpods, nuts, or dried berries, you will need another kind of base. Cut a circle out of corrugated cardboard or plywood to the size desired; cut out an inner circle. Attach materials with a strong glue (linoleum paste works well with heavy elements like pine cones). Be sure to cover the frame completely, and add a glue-on hanging device on the back.

A straw wreath can be constructed over a plastic foam base. (Plastic foam circles may be purchased at most craft and florist shops.) Pad the plastic foam with wads of newspaper, wrapping masking tape around the newspaper to hold it to the base. Lay bunches of straw around the base, wiring each bunch in place as you work; wrap with wire at every two inches until the base is completely covered. Add a hanging device.

Evergreen wreath. Use fine wire to attach greens to a circular frame.

Evergreen Wreath

Materials
evergreen branches
galvanized wire (4 to 6 feet)
spool of fine wire
wire cutter
ribbons, Christmas balls, holly sprig, or other decorative trim

Directions. Make a frame for the wreath by bending the galvanized wire into a circular shape and twisting the ends together.

Cut the evergreen branches into 8- or 10-inch lengths. Gathering one small bunch at a time, lay a bunch next to the wire frame; wire it to the frame with a few twists of the fine wire. Do not cut the fine wire after you have done this.

Lay another group of greens on top of the first. Secure this group with the wire and arrange the ends so that they overlap the first group slightly. Make sure you secure the greens firmly to the frame.

Continue around the frame in this manner, until the entire frame is covered with overlapping evergreens. Cut the wire and twist around the greens. At this point you can decorate the wreath with a ribbon bow, Christmas balls, a holly sprig, or any other decorations that please you. (Wire floral picks to cones and other stemless materials so they can be pushed into the wreath securely.)

Jute Wreath

Materials
4-ply jute (32 yards)
assorted dried flowers (zinnias, black-eyed Susans, statice, straw-
    flowers)
24-gauge aluminum wire
scissors
sturdy wire coat hanger

Directions. Bend the coat hanger into a circle shape. Cut eighty 14-inch lengths of jute. Fold each piece in half and mount on the coat hanger, using a lark's head mounting knot (see diagram). Unravel each ply of the jute, and then pull apart and fluff the jute. Push dried flowers into the wreath. Secure the flower stems to the coat hanger with 24-gauge wire.

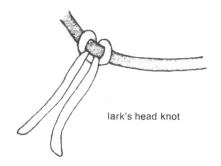

lark's head knot

Jute wreath. Fold each 14-inch length of jute in half and attach to frame with a lark's head mounting knot.

Evergreen wreaths can be decorated with strawflowers, pine cones, and ribbon.

The fluffy effect of this jute wreath was created by unraveling the jute. Dried zinnias, strawflowers, and statice add color and interest.

OTHER SPECIAL ARRANGEMENTS

Garlands, swags, and corsages make festive displays to celebrate parties, special occasions, and holidays throughout the year.

Garlands are built on a sturdy length of rope or cord and are flexible enough to be draped over doorways or mantels. You can make a loop in one end of the rope and tie it to a stationary object such as a door knob to make working easier. Group your materials in small bunches and attach them to the rope one at a time with wire, overlapping each group of materials as you work your way down the rope.

Swags are usually smaller than garlands. The base for a swag is often allowed to show as part of the design; ribbon makes a good base for swags of greens, grasses, or flowers. Cut several lengths of one- or two-inch-wide ribbon; bring the ends together and make an overhand knot. Cover the knot with a cone, a bow, or whatever else suits your design. Use wire to fasten your materials to the ribbon lengths.

Corsages can be used on almost any occassion. They do not have to be composed of fresh flowers and foliage, and they don't even have to be worn; for instance, a corsage of dried materials can be covered by a glass dome or used in a shadow box to make a charming display. One large piece or several smaller materials can be clustered to form the focal point, with ferns or other foliage for the background. Tape each individual stem with floral tape and then tape all the stems together. If the stems aren't sturdy, wind fine wire around each stem before taping. Add a small bow at the base of the corsage.

Swags. Fasten lengths of ribbon together, covering the knot with pine cones or a bow. Add small cones to ribbon ends.

Corsages. When using fresh flowers, snip the stems to 1 inch, add wire stems, and then wrap fresh stem ends with wet toweling before wrapping with floral tape. Arrange flowers, and then use tape to wrap all the stems together.

(Left) A fall swag, made by attaching dried flowers and glycerin-treated oak leaves to the leather straps of an old cowbell. Owned by Mary Tassava. (Above) Corsages can be made of dried or fresh flowers and foliage. (Below) An evergreen garland, decorated with bright bows and candy canes, makes a festive holiday display.

Organdy, silk, ribbon, lace, and beads were used to fashion this elegant bouquet by Margaret Shields. Handmade flowers can be lifelike or stylized, and may be crafted from a great variety of materials. The examples here and on the following pages suggest some of the possibilities.

Crafting Flowers

At those times of the year when fresh flowers are hard to come by, dried flowers, flowers preserved and used in prints or collages, and simulated flowers are especially welcome.

Flowers can be made out of almost anything, providing it can be cut or shaped to resemble a flower part. The most commonly used materials for making artificial flowers are paper, natural materials such as cones and seeds, and fabric. Your imagination and ingenuity will help you to find additional materials—and methods—for crafting flowers once you have become familiar with the basic process.

MATERIALS

Paper is an excellent material for making simulated flowers. It is inexpensive, easy to manipulate, and available in many colors and textures.

Crepe paper is a stretchy paper that can be pulled, crumpled, and cut into shape; it is available in a wide range of colors.

Tissue paper is a delicate paper that comes in as many, if not more, colors than crepe paper.

Kraft paper, the paper used for brown paper bags, is extremely sturdy. It can be purchased in colors too.

Wrapping paper, especially patterned paper, is available in great variety, and makes interesting and unusual flowers.

Foils, such as copper, brass, and aluminum foils used in tooling, and aluminum cooking foil, can be used to make striking metallic flowers.

Cellophane, transparent and slightly stiff, comes in a wide range of colors.

Newsprint, the soft, porous paper used for newspapers, is both cheap and easy to handle. You might even want to try using printed newspaper.

Tagboard is a heavy (but still pliable) paper available in white and most colors. It can be painted and used for leaves as well as petals.

As you learn to make flowers out of paper, you will undoubtedly discover other papers you can use as well.

Natural materials of many different kinds can be used in making flowers. The following are only a few of the possibilities.

Corncobs and husks can be used fresh or dried. Green husks can be cut into petal shapes and then allowed to dry. Dried corn husks should be soaked in water to make them pliable when you are ready to work with them. Cross sections of cobs, and corn silk, can be used for floral centers.

Onion skins can be used as flower petals (soak in water first).

Pine cones that have had their top ends sliced off resemble flowerlike shapes. The individual scales may be used as petals, secured to a flowerlike center with glue.

Seeds, especially the larger, flatter ones such as watermelon, squash, sunflower, and pumpkin seeds, can be used to form petals.

Fungi, found growing on trees, work well as petals.

Ideas for Flower Centers

You might try using:

- Actual dried flower centers, such as black-eyed Susans or daisies (reinforce the stems with wire while they are drying)
- Wads of soft paper (push 18-gauge wire stem into center, add white glue to hold) or cotton swabs
- Cross sections of corncobs or pine cones
- Clusters of seeds, coffee beans, corn kernels, or lentils, held together with glue (push wire stem or a length of doweling into cluster while glue is wet)
- Tiny pebbles or shells, bonded together with glue
- Thistles, seedpods, or bittersweet

Remember that simulated flowers do not have to be exact copies of real flowers. They may be stylized, following the dictates of your imagination, and the materials at hand. Consider trying some of the following combinations:

- Corn-husk petals with centers of black-eyed Susans
- Fabric petals with button or thimble centers
- Lace petals with a wad of fabric or a yarn pompon for a center
- Onion-skin petals with bittersweet centers
- Pumpkin-seed petals with thistle centers
- Pine-cone-scale petals with cross sections of corncobs as centers
- Newspaper petals with centers of crumpled wire
- Petals fashioned from wood shavings with sawdust (bonded with glue) centers
- Dried red-pepper petals with clusters of split peas as centers

Fabric. There's an enormous variety of fabrics on the market today, available in a wide range of colors, patterns, and textures. Sheer, stiff fabrics such as organdy work well in fabricating flowers: very little raveling occurs. Felt is another fabric that trims nicely with smooth, sharp edges. Some fabrics, such as batiste, do not have enough body to hold a petal shape, but this problem can be easily remedied. One solution is to iron interfacing onto the back of the fabric. Spray starch or sizing can also be used to give body to a fabric, and to prevent cut edges from fraying. (Years ago, people sometimes used sugar water for sizing. Today, you might try using a diluted white glue.) The list of fabric possibilities is almost endless—you're sure to find just the right one for the flowers you want to make.

Quilling—the art of curling narrow paper strips to form circles and other shapes—was used to make these delicate miniature flowers. By Betty Christy and Doris Tracy. (Courtesy of Craft Publications, Inc.)

(Left) These jaunty spring blossoms on painted wooden stems were made by Barbara Muccio. Cotton fabrics were used for two of the flowers; the daisy in the center was crocheted. (Below) There are many imaginative ways to use handcrafted flowers. A little basket filled with perky print-and-gingham flowers makes a party favor or a place-card holder. A grouping of baskets could serve as a table centerpiece. Gift packages can be decorated with fabric flowers and ribbons. By Diane Wagner.

(Right) Here, flowers made of cacti and thistles are arranged with bread sticks, spaghetti, and bleached ti leaves. (Below) This corsage, made of flowers crafted from corn husks and statice, is tied with a gay gingham bow.

GENERAL DIRECTIONS FOR ASSEMBLING FLOWERS

After you have decided what materials you will use and you have a rough idea of the kind of flowers you would like to make—that is, the size and shape of the petals, the size of the center, the length of the stem, the size and shape and quantity of the leaves—clear a working space for yourself and assemble your materials. You'll also need scissors, paper for petal and leaf patterns, white glue, 24-gauge wire for attaching parts, 18-gauge wire for stems, and floral tape. If you want to imitate a particular flower, have a few fresh ones—or a good picture—with you to use as a model.

1. If you're working with materials that can be cut and shaped, make a pattern of the petal shape on paper, and then transfer it to the petal material.

2. Cut out the petal shapes, varying the size slightly from petal to petal.

3. Decide what your floral center will be, and prepare it.

4. Attach the floral center to the stem (which may be a wire stem or a dried flower stem) by gluing and wiring them together.

5. Attach petals by putting a drop of glue on the end of each petal and pinching them to the flower center. Then wire all the petals in place around the base.

6. Wrap the base of the flower head and the stem with floral tape.

7. Cut out leaves and secure them to the stem with wire and tape.

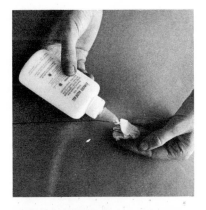
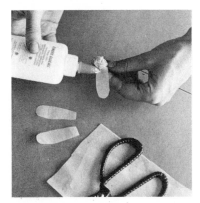

Attach floral center to stem by gluing and then wiring stem and center together. Attach each petal to center with glue.

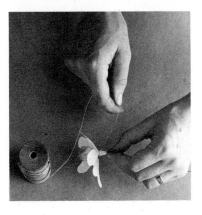

Securely wrap wire around petals and stem. Then, beginning at base of flower, wrap floral tape all the way down the stem.

Waxed Daisies and Daffodils

Materials

1 package yellow crepe paper
1 package tracing paper
18-gauge aluminum wire
24-gauge aluminum wire
dried daisy centers
yellow floral stamens (artificial)
floral tape
1 pound candle wax
white glue
acrylic paint (optional)

Directions. Use the patterns to cut daisy petals from the tracing paper and daffodil petals from the yellow crepe paper. Six petals are needed for each flower.

To make daisies. Dry real centers of daisies on their stems. Paint the centers with acrylic paint if they have faded. Glue 6 or 7 tracing-paper petals to each daisy center. Wire in place with 24-gauge wire. Wrap the base and stem with floral tape.

To make daffodils. Cut a 5-inch strip of crepe paper 2¾ inches wide. Pull and stretch one long edge of the crepe paper so that it ripples. Fold over ¼ inch of the rippled edge. Overlap the ends and glue them together. Gather the unrippled edge around a 12-inch length of 18-gauge wire. Use your fingers to push out the crepe paper so that a cuplike shape is formed. Lay 6 floral stamens inside the cup. Wire the cup onto the stem with 24-gauge wire. Glue and wire 6 petals around the cup, stretching the center of each petal slightly with your fingers. Wrap the base and stem with floral tape. Continue wrapping the floral tape down the stem.

Melt 1 pound of wax in a double boiler. The wax should be just at the melting point, not boiling. Dip the completed flowers in the wax. As the wax dries on the daffodils, shape the petals upward.

Arrange the daisies and daffodils (pictured on page 43) in an old ceramic pitcher or some other appropriate container. Baby's breath would be a good choice for fill.

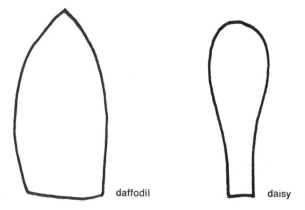

daffodil   daisy

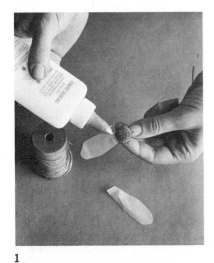

1

2

Waxed Daisies and Daffodils

1. To make daisies, glue paper petals to a dried daisy center.
2. Wire in place around the stem and then wrap stem with floral tape.

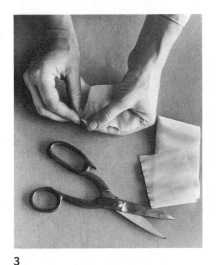

3

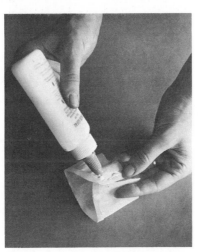

4

3. To make daffodils, pull and stretch one long edge of crepe paper so it ripples.
4. Bring short ends together and glue.

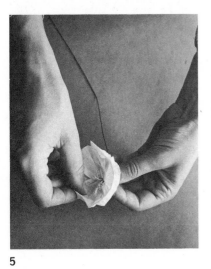

5

6

5. Gather unrippled edge around wire stem. Use your fingers to form a cup-like shape. Insert stamens and then wire cup in place on stem.
6. Glue and wire paper petals around the cup; wrap base and stem with floral tape.

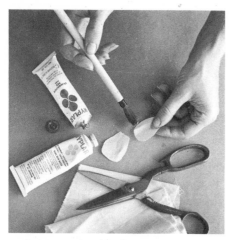

Color petals with diluted paint.

Tape petals to wire stem and continue wrapping down stem with tape.

Gather a doily around the flowers and tie with ribbon.

Nosegay of Pansies and Violets

A nosegay is a small bunch of flowers gathered together and tied with a ribbon. A doily is often used to frame the flowers.

Materials

lilac, yellow, and green percale fabric (⅛ yard each)
½-inch-wide lilac and yellow ribbon (½ yard each)
purple acrylic paint
artist's paintbrush
18-gauge aluminum wire (42 inches)
yellow floral stamens (artificial)
floral tape
crocheted doily (6-inch diameter)

Directions. Using violet pattern, cut 55 petals from the lilac percale. Dilute the paint slightly with water, and paint each petal separately.

Cut 12 pansy petals from the yellow percale. Paint them from the outside edge toward the center. Leave a rim of yellow unpainted to make the petal appear more pansylike.

Cut 8 leaves out of the green percale.

While the petals are still slightly damp, form them into flowers. Cut fifteen 6-inch lengths of 18-gauge wire for the stems. Use floral tape to fasten 4 stamens to the end of each wire. With your fingers, pinch 4 or 5 violet petals to 11 stems. Add leaves to some of them. Use 3 petals for each of the 4 pansies. Tape petals (and leaves) to each stem and continue wrapping the floral tape down the stem. Allow the flowers to dry.

Bring the flowers together in a bunch. Push the stems through the center of the doily. Gather up the doily around the flowers and tie securely with ribbon.

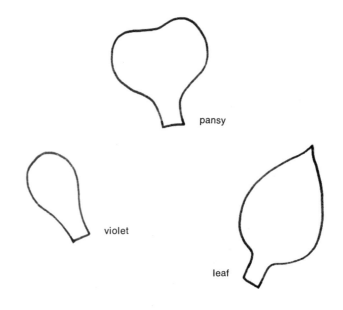

pansy

violet

leaf

An old-fashioned nosegay of fabric violets and pansies, framed by a crocheted doily

The transparent quality of these paper daisies and daffodils was achieved by dipping them in wax. Instructions are given on page 40.

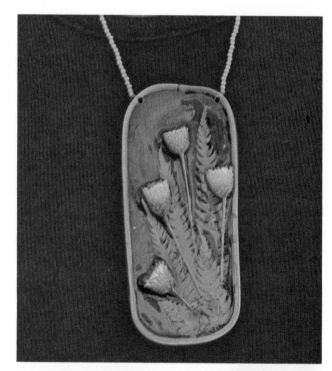

Dried flowers and foliage, embedded in plastic resin and framed with lead came, make delightful "Sun Catchers" (below) and a handsome pendant (right). By Bette Ball.

Embedding Flowers in Plastic

Dried flowers and leaves can be embedded in a clear plastic resin, permanently preserving their full color and form, to make delightful paperweights, plaques, and ornaments. The basic method is quite simple: the flowers are placed in a mold, which is then filled with liquid plastic, poured in layers. When the plastic has hardened, it is removed from the mold and the edges of the piece are buffed smooth.

Liquid plastic resin for embedding, available at craft stores, comes in two containers: one holds the casting resin itself, and the other a hardening catalyst that must be added just before pouring. The ratio of hardening agent to resin depends on the brand, but is usually anywhere from one to ten parts hardener to one hundred parts liquid plastic resin. Be sure to follow the directions on the package you buy. (Transparent dyes may be added to the resin for color, but since they tend to detract from the natural look of the flowers, they aren't recommended.)

Molds in various sizes and shapes can be purchased at craft stores, or they can be made from containers found around the house. Liquid plastic resin can be used with glass, wood, metal, or plaster-of-paris molds. However, it will dissolve some plastics, so if you want to use a plastic mold, be sure to test it first. (Place a drop of resin on the mold; if it doesn't turn sticky after ten to fifteen minutes, it can be used.) In looking for possible molds around the house, remember that you want to get the embedment out of the mold once the liquid plastic has hardened; containers that are wider at the top than at the bottom are easiest to unmold. You might consider small muffin tins, gelatin molds, or custard cups. Disposable molds can also be used—for instance, a small glass jar can be gently broken to release an embedment.

Directions. Have all your materials ready before you begin. Prepare your mold by coating the inside with a commercial mold release, paste wax, floor wax, or beeswax for ease in unmolding.

Following package directions, mix the exact quantities of resin and catalyst needed for the first layer of plastic (which will be *under* your flowers or leaves). Use a glass bowl and stir carefully with a glass rod or wooden stick. Let mixture stand for a minute or two so air bubbles can escape.

Pour mixture into mold until it reaches the level at which you want the flowers. Allow this first layer of resin to harden slightly; it should be about as firm as set gelatin. (Test with a stick—not your finger.) Then carefully add the flowers. After the base layer of resin has fully hardened, add more resin, one layer at a time as package instructions specify, until mold is filled to the depth desired. Let set for 24 hours.

Tips. Pour resin into one corner of the mold, just a little at a time. Heat is produced by the chemical reaction between catalyst and resin; pouring a little at a time reduces excess heat and avoids cracking. Look for air

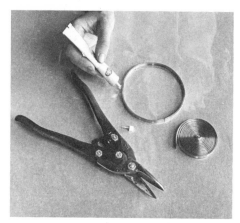

Shape a mold from lead came and glue to Mylar.

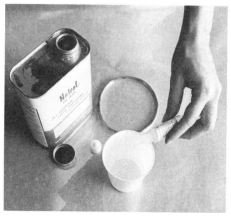

Mix catalyst and casting resin.

Quickly pour in a 1/16-inch layer. Let dry slightly. Mix another batch and pour over flowers.

bubbles, especially around the flowers, and use a toothpick to pop any that appear.

Finishing. Remove embedment from mold and polish it, beginning with a coarse grade of sandpaper and working to a finer grade. Finish with a metal-polishing paste applied with a soft rag.

Sun Catchers

Materials
a sheet of Mylar
lead came (type used for stained glass)
liquid casting resin and catalyst
glass bowl
stirring rod
sharp knife or single-edged razor blade
Duco cement
tape
board
dried flowers and ferns
drill
plastic leader

Directions. Tape Mylar on board. (Board should be large enough to accommodate one or more of the sun catchers.) Cut lead came to desired lengths and shape into circles or ovals.

Cement the lead came shapes to the Mylar, making sure all edges are sealed, to make molds for the resin.

Following package directions, mix resin with the catalyst. Mix only enough for one pouring.

Pour mixture into each lead-came mold to a depth of 1/16 inch. Move resin around with a stick to spread it evenly over the entire bottom surface of each mold. Let dry slightly.

Arrange flowers in molds. Mix another batch of resin and pour over flowers, making sure all the flowers are coated and resin meets the edge of each mold. Allow to dry until hard.

Peel Mylar from sun catchers, clean off edges, and drill holes on top for hanging. Hang with plastic leader in a low-light window to reduce fading.

Collage and Decoupage

COLLAGE

A collage is an overlapping arrangement of assorted materials. Dried flowers, foliage, and other natural materials, as well as fabricated ones, can all be used to make interesting and attractive collages. Collages can be used to make framed "pictures," notepapers, or place cards; they can be displayed under glass domes or mounted, uncovered, on any number of unusual backgrounds.

The surface you use for mounting your collage can be as informal as an old weathered board or a sheet of sandpaper, or as formal as velvet or silk framed in gilt. If your collage is to be an informal one that won't be framed under glass, you can use almost any kind of plant material that you have preserved according to the directions on pages 8 to 13. If you plan to frame your collage under glass, use only pressed materials prepared according to the directions on page 9.

Pressed flowers and weeds, arranged under glass and framed with weathered wood. By Betty Carey Glissendorf.

Glue fabric around cardboard backing cut to size of frame opening.

To make a flat, framed collage, assemble your pressed flowers and leaves, white glue, your frame, stiff cardboard, and your background material—fabric or paper. Cut the cardboard so that it just fits inside your frame. If you are using paper as a background, cut it to the size of the cardboard and then glue it to the cardboard. If you are using fabric, cut it so that it is about a half inch larger, all around, than the board. Glue the overlapping edges of the fabric to the back of the cardboard.

After you have decided how to arrange your flowers and foliage, glue them in place. Use a toothpick to apply just a small dab of glue for each piece in the collage. Allow the glue to dry, and then place the collage in the frame.

If you have a domed glass frame or a deep shadow box, or if you want to mount the arrangement on something like an old board or a piece of driftwood, you do not have to restrict yourself to flat materials when making your collage. You can use materials preserved by hanging or with glycerin or granular drying agents—or you can use crafted flowers and foliage. Prepare the background as described above if you are using one, and then arrange the preserved or fabricated flowers and foliage on it, gluing them in place carefully. Use more glue (or even linoleum paste) on heavier materials. Allow the collage to dry thoroughly before standing it upright or covering it with glass.

Here, a shadow box makes an interesting setting for a collage of preserved flowers.

(Top left) These clever note-card designs by Irene Harms are made of dried and dyed seedpods. (Bottom left) Fungi form the petals for crafted flowers arranged on a piece of driftwood. By Don Larsen. (Below) Dyed and natural seedpods were used to make the flowers in this collage designed by Irene Harms.

DECOUPAGE

Decoupage is the art of decorating surfaces with applied paper cutouts and then covering them with a transparent finish such as varnish or lacquer.

Pressed flowers can be used to beautiful effect in this simplified adaptation of the basic techniques.

The surface you choose can be wood (pre-painted or stained), metal, glass, plaster, or wax. You might consider decorating a wooden box, a metal tray, an old coffeepot, a small plaque, a candle, or even a piece of driftwood.

The materials you will need are: pressed flowers and foliage, acrylic gloss medium (available at craft stores), and a brush.

First, position the flowers and foliage on the object you've chosen (its surface should be clean and smooth). When you're pleased with the arrangement, lift up one flower at a time and brush a dab of gloss medium on the surface below it. Lay the flower back down on the wet area and brush gloss medium over it until it holds. When all the flowers and foliage are in place, brush the entire surface with a coat of acrylic gloss medium.

Let the first coat dry. Then add several more coats (allowing each one to dry thoroughly) until the flowers and leaves look as though they were embedded in varnish. (Acrylic gloss medium can be cleaned up with water while wet but dries to a hard, waterproof finish.)

To decoupage candles, proceed in the manner described above, covering the sides, but not the top, of the candle with coats of acrylic gloss medium.

(Facing page) These candles were decorated with pressed flowers, ferns, and leaves in a simplified adaptation of decoupage techniques. By Peggy Duca and Diane Wagner.

Printing with Flowers

Transfer printing. Dip flower in a puddle of ink or paint and then lay it, face down, on the printing paper.

The printing processes described here include transfer printing, spatter printing, and the making of shadograms. All of them are easy, and produce beautiful results. You can frame your prints, or use them as original greeting cards.

Transfer Printing

Transfer printing involves inking a fresh flower or leaf and then pressing it between two sheets of paper to obtain an image. Printing ink and India ink work quite well, as does liquid tempera paint. Almost any kind of absorbent paper can be used, including newsprint, kraft, bond, or rice paper.

First, choose a flower with a fairly flat head, such as a daisy, or a leaf with prominent veins, such as an ivy leaf. Squirt a puddle of ink or paint onto a pad of newspaper. Dip the flower or leaf face down in the ink. Then lay the inked flower or leaf, face down, onto the paper you are using for the print. Carefully lay another piece of paper on top of the first one and press the entire surface with the back of your hand, a large book, or a roller, if you have one. Then remove the inked flower or leaf and allow the print to dry.

If you want more than one image on the print, allow the first image to dry and then repeat the process, re-inking the same or another flower or leaf and placing it on the paper in another place.

Spatter Printing

Spatter printing makes use of pressed flowers or leaves as stencils. Ideally, you should use a mesh screen mounted on a wooden frame, but it is not strictly necessary.

First, lay the pressed material on the paper and fasten it down with straight pins. Lay the mounted screen over the paper. Then dip a stiff toothbrush in ink or tempera paint and rub it over the screen so that the ink spatters onto the paper and the flower beneath it. Remove the screen and lift the flower or leaf off the paper carefully. (If you do not have a screen, spatter the ink or paint by running your thumb down the head of a toothbrush. Clear a spacious working area for yourself and cover it with newspaper to catch spattered paint or ink.)

Allow the print to dry.

Spatter printing. Dip toothbrush in paint or ink and spatter over paper and pressed leaves by rubbing across surface of a raised screen.

Daisies and ferns were dipped in paint and then pressed between sheets of newsprint to make this colorful transfer print. By Diane Wagner.

Autumnal spatter prints by Diane Wagner. This technique can be used to create prints, greeting cards, and wrapping papers.

Shadowgrams

Shadowgrams are "photo prints" made without a camera that result in dramatic white-and-gray images on a black background. If you've had experience developing your own photographs, or if you have a friend who has developing facilities and is willing to help you, you may want to try making shadowgrams of pressed flowers or foliage.

Since numerous tasks must be performed in semi-darkness, and since timing is important, preparations should be made in advance and your equipment arranged conveniently to allow for a smooth flow of operations. Work in a space that can be completely darkened, or work at night. Cover windows with dark paper and place towels at the bottom of doors to avoid light leaks. Both a safelight (a low-wattage bulb with a special filter) and a regular light will be used at different times, so be sure they can be switched on independently. A nearby source of running water is a great convenience.

The equipment listed on page 55 is needed to make shadowgrams. The specialized items are available at photographic supply stores.

A simple frame makes an effective setting for a shadowgram.

Materials
2 metal or plastic trays, approx. 2 by 11 by 13 inches (for developer and stop bath)
3 metal or plastic trays, approx. 4 by 13 by 16 inches (for fixer, water, and hypo-clear)
print developer
stop bath
fixer (sometimes called hypo)
hypo-clear
safelight
gooseneck lamp with low-wattage bulb (optional)
photographic printing paper (8 by 10 inches is a good size)
2 tongs
a timer or a watch with a second hand
water source
measuring beaker
glass stirring rod
sponge
photographic print dryer (or spring-type clothespins and string or wire)

Making shadowgrams involves five procedures: preparing the photographic chemicals for use, arranging the flowers in a pleasing composition, and exposing, developing, and drying the prints.

Directions. To begin, place the trays in the order in which they will be used—for developer, stop bath, fixer, water, and hypo-clear. Prepare the film developer, stop bath, and fixer solutions according to the instructions on their labels. (These chemicals often come as powders and must be dissolved in water, although they can be purchased in ready-to-use form. Remember, always handle chemicals with care, keep them out of childrens' reach, and wash the mixing beaker and stirring rod between uses.) Prepare hypo-clear and water baths (water should be 70 degrees). Fill each tray about halfway with the appropriate solution. Be sure chemicals are all at room temperature when you use them.

Next, turn off the regular light and put on the safelight. Remove a sheet of printing paper from its light-proof container. Place it on a flat surface and arrange the pressed flowers on the light-sensitive emulsion side of the paper.

To create your shadowgram, turn on the regular light. This will expose the portions of the light-sensitive paper not covered by the flowers, and some light will be projected through the flowers. Experiment with different exposure times—from approximately 15 seconds to 1 minute—to get the best results. The time required will depend upon how opaque your flowers are and how intense your light source is. (For shadowgrams with sharper outlines, you might use a gooseneck lamp with a low-wattage bulb instead of a regular room light. Set the lamp so the bulb is a few feet above your paper.)

Turn off the regular light and turn on the safelight again.

Using tongs, completely submerge the exposed paper in the developing bath, moving it gently back and forth continuously for about 1 minute,

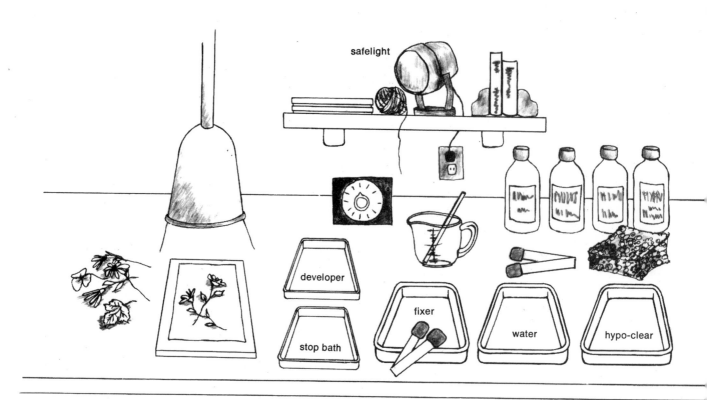

Shadowgrams. Prepare photographic chemicals and arrange trays in the order in which they will be used. Compose floral design. Then expose, develop, and dry the prints.

or until the background is deep black and the image is white. Remove it with the tongs and let the chemical bath drip-drain back into its tray. Then slip the print into the stop-bath tray, being careful not to let the tongs touch the liquid; use another tongs in the stop bath to agitate the print for 30 seconds. Then put the print into the fixer for 8 to 10 minutes. Next, put the print in the warm water bath (70° F.) for 30 seconds, and then put it in hypo-clear for 1 to 2 minutes. Finally, wash it under gently running water for 15 minutes or longer. (You can store a number of prints in the water tray and then rinse them all together in a sink or tub when you have completed your printing session. At this point in the process, prints can be exposed to regular light without causing damage.)

After washing, wipe prints with a sponge to absorb excess wetness and then dry on a photographic print dryer or hang from an overhead line or wire with spring-type clothespins. (Or wipe prints with a sponge every few minutes, turning them over each time, until they are completely dry.) When dry, press prints with a heavy weight for a few days to flatten them out.

To achieve the most interesting results with your shadowgrams, experiment with composition and overlapping, and try varying the exposure times.

Potpourris, Sachets, Pomanders, Powders, and Colognes

Before your fresh flowers begin to wilt, you can use the petals to make fragrant fresheners such as potpourri, sachet, cologne, or powder.

POTPOURRIS

Potpourri is a combination of flower petals, herbs, spices, and oils which are tossed together and stored in jars. Occasionally the lid of the jar is removed to allow its mellowed fragrance to permeate the room.

Potpourri is extremely easy to make. The basic recipe calls for one quart of dried flower petals and herb leaves, one teaspoon each of three or four different spices, one tablespoon of an essential oil, and one tablespoon of a fixative (to hold and blend the mixture).

Simply pull the petals from a variety of fragrant flowers and dry them on sheets of newspaper or screening to allow air circulation. Don't press them. Herbs should be dried by hanging, and then lightly crumbled with your fingers or a rolling pin.

For every quart of dried petals and herbs, add a tablespoon of essential oil to enrich the fragrance of your potpourri. Toss it lightly into the mixture. (Essential oils—essences extracted from plant sources—may be purchased from the suppliers listed on page 64, or you can make your own by following the directions on page 58. Do not use alcohol-based oils.)

One teaspoon each of three or four spices may also be added. Powdered spices such as cinnamon, ginger, or allspice work well. Lightly toss the mixture again.

Next, add one tablespoon of any of the fixatives, in powdered or oil form, that are suggested below. Toss the mixture once again and then store it in a stoppered glass jar for four to six weeks to age and mature.

Potpourri Materials

Flower Petals	Herbs	Fixatives	Spices	Essential Oils
lavender rose geranium lilac strawflower marigold roses honeysuckle 　and/or: patchouli sandalwood pine needles	basil mint rosemary lemongrass marjoram jasmine	orrisroot gum benzoin sage leaves musk civet ambergris	nutmeg vanilla beans allspice ginger cinnamon cloves	orange lemon lavender patchouli sandalwood

A Spicey Potpourri Recipe

Materials

1 cup rose petals
½ cup pine needles
½ cup marigold petals
½ cup strawflowers
½ cup mint leaves
½ cup basil
½ cup sage leaves
1 teaspoon cinnamon
1 teaspoon allspice
1 teaspoon cloves
1 tablespoon (½ ounce) oil of lemon
1 tablespoon orrisroot

Directions. Dry the flower petals and herbs thoroughly. Crumble them slightly. Toss in the spices and oil. The orrisroot and sage leaves will serve as fixative for the mixture. Store in a glass jar for 4 to 6 weeks.

SACHETS

Sachets are blends of dried flower petals, herbs, spices, and oils, too—enclosed in fabric and used to freshen lingerie and linens. Simply crumble a small amount of your favorite potpourri recipe and place the mixture in the center of a small square of fabric. Bring the corners of the material together and tie with ribbon or twine.

EXTRACTING ESSENTIAL OILS

There are two methods you can use at home to extract the volatile plant oils used in making potpourris, sachets, colognes, and powders.

For the first method, saturate cotton balls with mineral, olive, or saffron oil. In a glass jar, alternate layers of oiled cotton with flower petals. Herbs may also be used. Seal the jar tightly, and store in a warm place. After approximately one month, squeeze the oil from the cotton using a spoon as a press. Store the oil in a glass vial with a tight stopper.

For the second method, place one cup of mineral, olive, or saffron oil in the top part of a double boiler. Warm the oil, but don't bring it to the boiling point. Add flower petals or herbs to fill the pot, and cover. Allow the plants and oil to soak for about two hours over low heat, replacing the old plants with new ones approximately every half hour, until the oil has taken on the fragrance of the plants. Squeeze oil from the plants into the oil in the double boiler, strain, and store in glass, tightly covered.

POMANDERS

Pomander balls made from fruits are very popular and easy to make. Use an ice pick or other sharp instrument to cover an orange, lemon, lime, or apple with holes. Then press a whole clove into each hole and store in a dry place for a few weeks to mellow. (For added fragrance, the fruit can be stored in spices or a potpourri mixture.) As the fruit dries out, it will become very lightweight and fragrant. Tie the pomander with ribbon or gather it up in netting. Hang it for decoration, or use it to freshen the air in a closet.

(Left) Aromatic pomanders by Barbara Pond. (Below) Potpourri can be kept in glass jars, or used in sachets—like these by Marcia Larsen—to freshen closets and drawers.

Perfumed colognes and oils, made from fragrant flowers and herbs, are displayed to advantage in transparent bottles.

COLOGNES

Colognes can easily be made from fragrant flowers and herbs. Make your own essential oils, following the directions on page 58, and then use alcohol to extend them into a cologne. Use a glass container with a tight-fitting stopper or lid for mixing and storing. Cologne should be aged at least three or four months.

A Flowery Cologne Recipe

Materials
1 cup vodka
1 tablespoon (½ ounce) oil of lavender
1 tablespoon (½ ounce) oil of rose
1 tablespoon (½ ounce) oil of lilac

Directions. In a glass container, add the oils to the vodka and shake the mixture thoroughly. Store, tightly covered, in a dark place. Age at least 3 months, shaking the mixture once a day if possible.

POWDERS

You can make aromatic powders from scented flowers and herbs you've grown or collected yourself. Cornstarch is the basic ingredient, with flowers or herbs added for their fragrance. Lilacs, lily of the valley, and lavender make especially nice powders. When you package your homemade powders, they make delightful and personal gifts.

Spicey Bath Powder

Materials
1 pound cornstarch
1 teaspoon cinnamon
1 tablespoon (½ ounce) oil of lemon
fresh herbs (rosemary, sage)
shoebox lined with cloth or foil
cheesecloth

Directions. Blend cornstarch and cinnamon. Toss together with oil of lemon. Line a shoebox with cloth or foil and pour a ½-inch layer of the cornstarch mixture into the box. Lay a piece of cheesecloth over it. Place fresh herbs over the cheesecloth. Lay another layer of cheesecloth over the herbs. Add another ½ inch of cornstarch mixture. Continue alternating layers of cornstarch and herbs with cheesecloth until the box is full. Place the lid on the box. After 3 days, replace the plants with fresh ones. In a week or so, remove the plants and cheesecloth and let the powder dry.

To package your powder, cut off a circular oatmeal box to a height of 2¾ inches. Save the lid. Measure and cut a piece of pretty cotton print so it fits around the circumference of the box. Apply glue evenly to the outside of the box and carefully glue the fabric in place. Then apply glue to the inside of the box and fit precut fabric there, slitting where necessary to obtain a good fit.

Cut a circle of fabric 1½ inches larger than the cover. Apply glue to the top and the outside rim. Lay the fabric on the cover. Slit the overhanging edge every 3 inches or so. Apply glue to the inside of the rim and bend the fabric into place.

If desired, the box may be varnished with 8 to 10 coats of glossy wood varnish. Buy a powder puff, or make your own by following the directions below.

To crochet a powder puff, you'll need: 1 ounce white knitting worsted, a size H crochet hook, and ½ yard of ½-inch ribbon.

Chain 6 and join with slip stitch to form a ring. Work 10 sc into the ring. Work (2 sc in next sc, 1 sc in next sc) until piece measures 3½ inches in diameter. Then (work 2 sc in next sc, 1 sc in next 4 sc) until piece measures 5 inches, or about ½ inch smaller than the box. End with a slip stitch; cut and pull end through to finish.

Using the rya stitch, attach 4-inch lengths of yarn to rows of crochet, working from the center to cover the entire puff on both sides. Pull each strand of yarn through crochet, forming a loop. Pull ends through loop to knot. (See diagram.) Unravel the ends of the yarn and trim evenly. The cut rya stitches give the puff a soft pile surface. Make a ribbon bow and fasten to the center of the puff.

Using crochet hook to make a rya knot

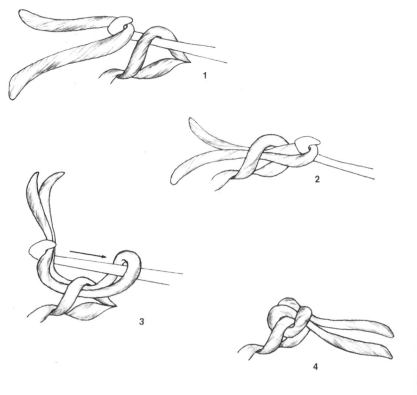

To make a fluffy puff, cover both sides of a crocheted circle with rya knots. Unravel all yarn ends, and then trim evenly for a pile effect.

Store Spicey Bath Powder in an apothecary jar. Or package it in a homemade fabric-covered box for gift-giving.

Bibliography

Bauzen, Peter and Susanne, *Flower Pressing,* Sterling Publishing Co., Inc., New York, 1971

Booke, Ruth Voorhees, *Pressed Flower Pictures.* Crown Publishers, Inc., Avenel Books, New York, 1972

Christy, Betty, and Tracy, Doris, *Miniature Quilled Flowers.* Craft Publications Inc., 1450 Kelton Dr., Stone Mountain, Georgia, 1976

Cutler, Katherine N., *How to Arrange Flowers for All Occasions.* Doubleday & Co., Inc., Garden City, New York, 1967

How to Arrange Fresh and Artificial Flowers. Beagle Manufacturing Co., Inc., 4377 No. Baldwin Ave., El Monte, California, 1968.

Love, Diane, *Flowers Are Fabulous: For Decorating.* The Macmillan Company, New York, 1975

Plummer, Beverly, *Fragrance: A Recipe Book.* Atheneum, New York, 1975

Squires, Mabel, *The Art of Drying Plants and Flowers.* Crown Publishers, Inc., Bonanza Books, New York, 1968

Underwood, Raye Miller, *The Complete Book of Dried Arrangements.* Crown Publishers, Inc., Bonanza Books, New York, 1970

Westland, Pamela, and Critchley, Paula, *The Art of Dried and Pressed Flowers.* Crown Publishers, Inc., New York, 1974

Suppliers

Most of the tools and materials mentioned in this book are readily available at local florist shops, garden centers, and large department and hardware stores. Special items may be ordered from the suppliers listed below; in some instances, a charge will be made for their catalog.

**Preserving Materials
and Floral Supplies**
Cook's Crafts
202 North Ct.
Dixon, IL 61021

Lee Wards
Creative Crafts Center
1200 St. Charles St.
Elgin, IL 60120

Floral Art
P.O. Box 1985
Springfield, MA 01101

Boycan's Craft Supplies
P.O. Box 897
Sharon, PA 16146

Materials for Plastic Embedding
Bergen Arts & Crafts
P.O. Box 381
Marblehead, MA 01945

American Handicrafts
1011 Foch
Ft. Worth, TX 76107

Herbs, Spices, Oils
The Herbary and Potpourri Shop
P.O. Box 543
Childs Homestead Rd.
Orleans, MA 12653

Caswell-Massey Co., Ltd.
320 West 13th St.
New York, NY 10014

P. Fioretti & Co., Inc.
1470–2 Lexington Ave.
New York, NY 10028

Nichols Garden Nursery
1190 North Pacific Hwy.
Albany, OR 97321

Papers for Crafting Flowers
Dick Blick
P.O. Box 1267
Galesburg, IL 61401

Dennison's Party Bazaar
390 Fifth Ave.
New York, NY 10018
Attention: Mr. Wexler

Bleached ferns and painted artichokes were used to form this tall, vertical design.